DECLUTTER YOUR MIND

Dr. Talya Miron-Shatz and the Buddy&Soul team

INTRODUCTION: WELCOME TO DECLUTTER YOUR MIND

You want to feel empowered. You want to live with clarity and peace of mind. But sometimes you find you might be weighed down by mental clutter, negative thoughts, and a general sense of being reoccupied and feeling overwhelmed. You can't move forward without first doing some emotional digging. This course will help you tackle some of your negative thoughts, harmful biases, unpleasant emotions, and stinging memories that are making you wonder why you can't focus, while hogging prime real estate in your mind. So, lighten your load and make space for a mind free of mental clutter, anxiety, stress, or feeling overwhelmed with life. Clutter free mind, here we come!

There are three goals that we had in mind while creating this book. We want you to:

- Identify what's cluttering your mind, and why.

- Let go of negative thoughts, emotions, memories, and even people.

- Approach life with increased clarity, serenity, inner peace, and peace of mind.

Simply put, decluttering is the process of pruning away unnecessary items. When we're talking about mental and emotional decluttering, it means pruning away anything that makes us less effective or less happy than we could be. We usually think of decluttering as a physical process, but it is equally important when we're talking about decluttering our minds.

Think of all the thoughts, expectations and even people that are clogging up your mental and emotional space. If not dealt with, these can sometimes become a permanent state of mind and a part of who you are. You may not even notice it anymore; maybe you've forgotten what it's like to *not* have endless mental to-do lists. To not have worries, nags, and small things that keep getting filed and refiled for later, and later still.

Mental decluttering may not come intuitively to everyone, but we believe that it is a basic skill that is worth learning. It can re-infuse your life with the kind of positive energy that will allow you to become the person you strive to be.

Decluttering your mind is part of a larger picture of mental health and wellbeing and you are cordially invited to join us for the process.

Make room for what matters – and gain clarity, mental energy, inner peace, and peace of mind along the way.

YOUR JOURNEY TO DECLUTTERING YOUR MIND

INTRODUCTION: Welcome to Declutter Your Mind	Page 2
How to Use This Book	Page 4
Why I Created Buddy&Soul	Page 5
STRATEGY 1: Know why you're here	Page 6
STRATEGY 2: Start small	Page 13
STRATEGY 3: Tackle your to-dos	Page 20
STRATEGY 4: Banish stress	Page 27
STRATEGY 5: Close your expectation gap	Page 34
STRATEGY 6: Declutter people in your life	Page 41
STRATEGY 7: Declutter your false beliefs	Page 49
STRATEGY 8: Make amends with the past	Page 56
STRATEGY 9: Declutter "floater moments"	Page 63
STRATEGY 10: Experience your newfound peace of mind	Page 71
Where Do We Go From Here	Page 78

HOW TO USE THIS BOOK TO DECLUTTER YOUR MIND

In this book you'll find ten great strategies for achieving the goals we listed above. You'll also find inspiring content and exercises you can engage with to help you practice decluttering your mind.

You will get the most out of this book by going through the strategies and associated exercises one by one. Of course, you can also simply read it the whole way through. But we recommend using this book by going through it in order, watching the TED talks, and doing the exercises. We have found the best way to do the exercises is by dedicating a notebook as your course journal. If you're reading this book on a PC, feel free to create a text file and use that as your course journal. Or you could simply use a good ol' pen and paper to do the exercises. Either way, we recommend keeping some method of writing handy while you go through the exercises in this book to optimize what you get out of it.

To maximize your experience with the Buddy and Soul book, share your thoughts and insights with us on social media! Post pictures relating to your progress on Instagram and Twitter, tagging @Buddy_N_Soul, and Facebook @Buddy&Soul. By sharing with us on social media, not only can you help others with their personal journeys, you can read about those facing similar challenges.

Direct message us YOUR story @Buddy_N_Soul on Instagram and be anonymously featured for a chance to **win a Buddy&Soul three month free membership**.

If you really want to go all the way, visit our website, BuddynSoul.com, and explore all that we have to offer beyond 'Declutter Your Mind'. In fact, we have three other books in the wellness series that we think you might benefit from: Stress Management, Cultivating Authentic, Willpower 101

WHY I CREATED BUDDY&SOUL AND HOW I WORK ON DECULTTERING MY MIND

I'm Dr. Talya Miron-Shatz, CEO of Buddy&Soul, where Declutter Your Mind and many more e-courses and books come from. I have a PhD in psychology and was very fortunate to do my post-doc at Princeton University with Nobel Laureate Daniel Kahneman. I've also taught at the Wharton Business School, University of Pennsylvania. Now I'm a professor at the Ono Academic College, and a visiting researcher at Cambridge University. I used to study happiness, and for a long time now, I've been studying medical decision making and helping organizations support people on their way to joy and health. One thing that struck me as unfair was that we were expecting people to change their life for good but weren't giving them the tools to do so. People deserve all the help they can get when breaking out of old patterns and moving their lives forward.

This is what Buddy&Soul does.

We support you in many ways by providing science-based actionable ways to sustain your body and mind. We help you sleep better, spark a change in your eating habits, and manage stress. We teach you how to create new habits and how to engage your willpower. We help you grow, claim your self-esteem, cultivate authenticity, reframe your life story, achieve your goals and so much more including decluttering your mind.

We created unique course clusters for people dealing with specific challenges: students, patients, and pregnant women.

Everything you need to change your life for good.

I want to hear from YOU! Please feel free to send me an email with your thoughts, suggestions, and feedback regarding this book to talya@buddynsoul.com. I would love to hear what you think about this book and how it helped you with decluttering your mind. Your feedback is extremely valuable and will allow us to help more individuals, like yourself, to obtain the necessary tools and support needed to change their lives for good.

STRATEGY 1: Know why you're here

Sometimes, we want to (or have to) do something important but can't motivate ourselves to do it. Especially when we're dealing with something vague like emotional clutter. We're not sure where to begin and we may doubt the bottom-line value of the endeavour in the first place. This is especially true if it you're trying to accomplish something abstract; it will likely sit on the back burner for longer than you intend.

Clarifying what's motivating you to declutter your mind is the first step towards moving your goal from abstract to concrete and of course, to making it happen. **Your initial motivation is something you can revisit when the going gets rough.** If you ventured into Declutter Your Mind, there had to be a reason, and this reason will sustain your commitment as you work your way through the course. So why not spell it out?

(Plus: Check out our Achieve Your Goals course.)

One great way to do this is with a technique that psychologists call motivational interviewing (MI). Motivational interviewing means asking yourself those really hard questions about why you want to make a change in your life – not why your significant other or best friend or mom wants you to make a change, but why *you* want to make a change. In their 2008 MI guide for clinicians, Sobell and Sobell explain that "change talk tends to be associated with successful outcomes. This strategy elicits reasons for changing from clients by having them give voice to the need or reasons for changing" (p. 1). In other words, **you determine for yourself what's motivating you to make a change – in this case to declutter your mind** – instead of having someone spoon-feed you "the right" answers. Research has found this to be an effective step of lasting behavioral change.

(Plus: Check out our Tackling Change course).

Some MI questions you can start this course with, based on the suggestions of Sobell & Sobell (p.1) are:

- "What would you like to see different about your current situation?"
- "What makes you think you need to mentally and emotionally declutter?"
- "What will happen if you don't declutter your mind and emotions?"
- "What would be the good things about clearing your mental clutter?"
- "Suppose you don't change, what is the WORST thing that might happen?"
- "What is the BEST thing you could imagine that could result from changing?"
- "If you make changes, how would your life be different from what it is today?"
- "How would you like things to turn out for you in 2 years?"

Let the private interview begin!

DRIVING THE MESSAGE HOME

I'm glad that you've decided to join us for the Declutter Your Mind course. Each session of our course consists of a warm-up talk followed by a hands-on component where you'll learn a new skill or idea and have a chance to start putting it into action.

We're going to start the Declutter Your Mind course by taking a fundamental look at why we should take on this challenge in the first place.

Decluttering your mind is about being brutally honest with yourself: your needs, wants, beliefs, the people around you, regrets, stresses and your productive time. It might bring up all sorts of emotions and worries you buried a long time ago. Now you can address those feelings once and for all.

Who knows what your motivation to emotionally declutter is? Only you! And sometimes you have to dig deep inside yourself to find your reason. Listen to Carrie Green talk about things that might be stopping you. Carrie felt off-kilter with self-limiting beliefs and in order to be successful she had to figure out what achievement meant to her. She had to program her mind for success. She controlled her thoughts rather than allowing them to control her.

We think you'll find that the more you put into the course, the more you'll get out of it. So take full advantage of all our features and find your place in a community of people facing similar challenges.

Enjoy!

Watch 'Programming Your Mind For Success' presented by Carrie Green at TEDxManchester on YouTube.

EXERCISE

Practice motivational interviewing to help you get really specific about why you're here, in the Declutter Your Mind course. Take the role of both the interviewer and the interviewee and write your honest responses to some of the questions we listed above. Here are 3 to get you started. Read them carefully, and use your journal to write down the answers with the utmost honesty:

- What makes you want to declutter your mind?
- What positive outcomes do you hope to gain from this course?
- What will happen if you don't make a change?

TIPS

Tip 1: Feeling stuck? Imagine sitting in front of an interviewer who listens, raises an eyebrow, and asks "What aren't you telling me" until you get to the bottom of your motivation.

Tip 2: No judgment here, and no censorship. Just be brutally honest and promise to forgive yourself for whatever comes out!

What's motivating you to declutter your mind?

Decluttering your mind is hard work! It is one of those tasks that take hard work and motivation. What are some of the things motivating you to declutter your mind?
(Plus: Check out our Priorities Reboot and Achieve Your Goals courses.)

1. I can't think straight anymore because my mind is so chaotic.
2. I want to have more Zen in my life.
3. I heard about this course from a friend and he raved about the benefits.
4. I have no other option.
5. I want to have more clarity in my thinking.
6. I want something to change in my life, so I figure why not start with my mind?

Did we miss anything? Add it in your journal: _____

I can't declutter my mind without professional help

Double-edged sword, here. You've convinced me that this is important, but isn't it so important that I should seek professional help?

For:

1. If someone's going to be playing around in my mind, they should have a license to do so.
2. Some of the things that are weighing on me go way back. I don't think I should just haphazardly chuck them out.
3. A professional can help me decipher what (and who) needs to go, and what should stay. I can't make those calls on my own.

Add you own argument:

4. _____

Against:

1. A professional can only show you the way. The actual decluttering will always be exclusively up to you.
2. For big things, maybe it's best to seek a professional. But for things like returning a scarf from 3 years back, those can be tackled now and done with forever!
3. Seeking professional help is almost always a smart move, if you can afford it and have the time and the means for it. But there are steps you can take alone, based on how you feel, that can do a great deal of the work for you.

Add you own argument:

4. _____

The unexpected motivator that helped me declutter my mind

Decluttering your mind is a blessed venture, but it's not always easy or intuitive. What kept you motivated when things got tough or real life emergencies tried to keep you from your goal? Share with the community, and help inspire others to keep at it! Spend five minutes writing about such an experience you've had recently in your 'Declutter Your Mind' journal.

Direct message us YOUR story @Buddy_N_Soul on Instagram and be anonymously featured for a chance to **win a Buddy&Soul three month free membership**.

13 Miracles that happen when you declutter your mind

You've worked so hard on emotional decluttering, and now you see the results.

1. Finally, your head will feel quiet.
2. You will be able to control your thoughts, instead of the other way around.
3. Even though your sister's a doctor and you are "only" a teacher (as your older car and smaller home can also testify), you'll finally have fun having dinner with her, knowing she loves and admires you for who you are.
   (Plus: Check out our Defining your Identity course.)
4. You'll develop your ability to really listen to yourself, becoming your own teacher and guide.
   (Plus: Check out our Cultivating Authenticity course.)
5. You'll become your own cheerleader, not needing anyone else's approval.
6. You will embrace letting go.
7. You'll become more self-aware.
8. When you see other people who have taken time to work on themselves in the same deep way, they'll stand out to you. You will be able to identify each other as 'members of the club.'
9. You will notice all kinds of good characteristics and traits in yourself that you might never have noticed. It'll be like meeting someone new.
10. You'll be more emotionally present – less things taking up your mental space gives you more room to focus on the present.

Add your items to the list:

11. _____

12. _____

13. _____

STRATEGY 2: Start small

Declutter my mind, huh? Let's start with a baby step before we dive in. **This is the best way to convince you that mental clutter exists and that clearing it up is not only possible, but needed.**

Personal example: a friend and I used to go to a yoga studio together. Once, just before the studio closed down, she paid for my class out of her 10-class ticket. I never paid her back. She must have forgotten it, and would probably shake it off if I mentioned it, but every now and then, it would cross my mind and bother me. It was always lurking, taking up precious RAM from my limited supply of mental energy. Why not pay her and move on with my life?

In his book *Clearing Emotional Clutter: Mindfulness Practices for Letting Go of What's Blocking Your Fulfillment and Transformation*, Donald Altman, psychotherapist and former Buddhist Monk, compares the process of emotional decluttering to emptying the trash on your computer hard drive. With all those extra files in the background your computer runs a lot slower. If you take the time to delete those extra files one by one, your computer will speed up (p. 6).

What's using up your mental energy? Do you owe someone something? An apology? Money? A thank you card or some other type of acknowledgement? An explanation for why you didn't do something they expected you to do? Do you need to finally return that shawl you borrowed six months ago, or explain to your co-worker that you got a nasty stomach virus and could not come to his son's Christening, and finally give them their gift (true story)? Take some time to follow through on the thought and then delete it from your brain's hard drive.

This session is about getting your feet wet with a teeny tiny emotional declutter trial run. Identify something that's weighing on you, take care of it, and feel recharged with mental energy as you take a deep breath and forget about it forevermore!

DRIVING THE MESSAGE HOME

Hello again, we're glad you're back because you don't want to miss this one! Do you know yourself well enough? If asked to list what you owe and to whom, could you do it quickly? And if so...what took you so long to get around to doing it?

Procrastination doesn't make sense. In this hilarious talk, Tim Urban takes us on a journey through YouTube binges, Wikipedia rabbit holes and bouts of staring out the window. Ponder what you are really procrastinating on: who do you need to thank or apologize to? Use your rational decision-making skills to get those things out of your head. Don't be a spectator in your own life, stay away of the instant gratification monkey and get these jobs out of your head! Do the action; feel great.

Watch 'Inside the Mind of a Master Procrastinator' presented by Tim Urban on YouTube.

EXERCISE

Step 1: **Identify something that's nagging at you and weighing on your mind. Unsure what it is? Close your eyes and imagine total peace of mind. You might notice something bothering you.** Write it down in your journal.

Step 2: **Commit to an action you will take to get it off your mind, and set a time this week for getting it done**. Make that phone call, return that book, or send in those forms to the insurance company. Phew. Can you feel the energy freeing up, and some peace of mind setting in?

TIPS

Tip 1: The trick here is to pick something relatively small that's weighing on your mind – something that can be tackled and crossed off the to-do list in one sitting.

Tip 2: Fun having it off your chest? Upload a photo, video, or story illustrating how this mini-declutter worked out for you.

Tip 3: Not sure where to start? Check out our Priorities Reboot course.

Which traits make it hard for you to declutter?

What traits do you recognize in yourself that make decluttering (bad) friends or false beliefs difficult to do?

1. People-pleasing.
2. Sense of justice.
3. Friendliness: I need people!
4. Anxiety. I can't get out of my own head.
5. Stubbornness. It's really hard to admit I was wrong!

Add your own: _____

7 Ways to deliver a long-awaited apology

You've finally decided to make that long overdue apology… But how? If you've waited too long and you now fear it could be awkward, here are a few ways to go about getting that apology to its rightful owner.

1. Text, or email it. While not an ideal method of communication, giving a written apology allows you to think in advance of what you want to say, and to avoid having to stand there while the other person processes it.
2. Elaborately. If you turn the apology into a big to-do, you'll be able to get over your embarrassment a little more easily. No need to hire a marching band, but even a balloon or a festive coffee offering will help mitigate your distress.
3. With a mediator. Having a third-party there can help you overcome your quite understandable wish to avoid the whole scenario.

Add your items to the list:

4. _____

5. _____

6. _____

The mini-step that helped me declutter my mind

There's so much clutter that bangs around in our mind, that it's hard to know where to start if we want to clear the mess. What was the small step that allowed you to get started on the process of decluttering your mind? Spend five minutes writing about such an experience you've had recently in your 'Declutter Your Mind' journal.

Direct message us YOUR story @Buddy_N_Soul on Instagram and be anonymously featured for a chance to **win a Buddy&Soul three month free membership**.

Decluttering my mind is a waste of time

I could cross off half my to-do list in all that time spent fixing my head. Mind-decluttering is a game for those who have time to play.

For:

1. A waste of time indeed. Not only will you not be able to cross things off your to-do list in the time you spend contemplating your own self, but you'll be adding more items to it!
2. If I can't sleep from too much brain activity, I'll just pop a pill. Simple as that.
3. I've been functioning just fine until now. No need to push myself so far beyond my comfort zone.

    Add you own argument:

4. _____

Against:

1. Waste of time!? Try sage investment! Every minute, hour, or day you put into emotional decluttering yields huge payoff.
2. Taking pills helps you tonight, but what happens 10 years down the road when you are still losing sleep because you are stuck on the very same emotional merry-go-round? Will you just keep taking sleeping pills forevermore?
   (Plus: Check out our Sleep Well course.)

    Add you own argument:

3. _____

STRATEGY 3: Tackle your to-dos

Do you ever wake up in the middle of the night remembering something you had to do, meant to do, never got around to, should do, could do, or would do? Just like ragged shirts and broken chairs can make your house overcrowded, **endless to-dos, loose ends to tie, worries, and things you wanted to do but never got around to, can easily clutter your mental space,** leaving you feeling overwhelmed.

(Plus: Check out our Priorities Reboot course.)

"Getting stuff done" takes courage (yes, courage) and a big push – but it's worth it. The beautiful Amy K. is my model for tackling the do-do list. We used to work together at Princeton University. I was a young researcher and she was a much younger research assistant, a Princeton graduate, who totally had her act together. You could not miss this about her. She would use her breaks to pay her bills in her neat handwriting, with stamps she carefully kept in her purse. Not only was she always immaculately dressed and her desk Ikea catalogue-esque, but you could almost see how clear her mind was. When I need to tackle my to-dos, I bring Amy's image to mind, envisioning how put-together she is, and I strive to emulate her qualities. Suddenly, it becomes easier.

In a famous time management lecture given by the late Carnegie Melon Computer science professor Randy Pausch, who at the time was dying from pancreatic cancer, offers useful strategies for dealing with tedious to-dos. One of my favorite moments is when Pausch asks, "What will happen if I don't do it?" His response? "The best thing in the world is when I have something on my To Do list and I just go: *Hmm, no. No one has ever come and taken me to jail*" (Pausch, p.5). If it's not so important, drop it. And then it's one less thing on your mind and on your to-do list.

Another helpful strategy comes from David Allen's bestseller *Getting Things Done: The Art of Stress-Free Productivity*. It's called the two-minute rule and it goes like this: "If an action will take less than two minutes, it should be *done* at the moment it is defined" (p. 35). That means that anything that will take under two minutes shouldn't even make it onto the to-do list in the first place. Just get up and do it. Getting that list down is the first step to getting it off your mind and doesn't actually take very long.

DRIVING THE MESSAGE HOME

Hi, how did you feel when you woke up this morning? Like you had a million and one things to do? For that matter, could you fall asleep with all your responsibilities whispering evil nothings into your ear? The next action will focus on helping you clear your mind of all those petty little things that you have to do in life (i.e., everything). Making a list is an excellent step towards motivating yourself to do what needs to be done and be able to let it go. Nothing feels quite as good as finishing an annoying task and knowing you never have to think about it again (until the next time you have to change the kitty litter, at least).

But behind the to-do list stands the big gray notion of motivation. Watch this fascinating TED Talk by Dan Pink about motivation, and maybe learn a new way to get yourself motivated towards decluttering your mind and reclaiming some of that mental energy.

Watch 'The Puzzle of Motivation' presented by Dan Pink on YouTube.

EXERCISE

Use your journal to make a **list of all the nagging things you need to take care of on the practical front,** big or small. E.g., get a new memory card to replace the one I lost for my mom's electronic picture frame, renew my passport, get rid of mismatched socks clogging up my drawer, or sign up for the gym.

Then review your list and **cross off anything that is unrealistic, unnecessary, or simply doesn't belong there**. Once finalized, think of your list as a contract and get to it.

TIPS

Tip 1: Chances are some of these things have been on your mind for a while. Don't overthink them. Don't agonize over them. Dive in – and do them! In fact, see if you can cross something off the list right now.

Tip 2: Revisit your list in your journal on a regular basis. You can always add, delete, and modify as needed.

Tip 3: To turn decluttering your mind into a habit, be sure to check out our Habit Workshop course.

13 ways to overcome your difficulties in decluttering your mind

Starting to emotionally declutter is sometimes the hardest part. Once you get past that initial barrier, you'll be surprised at how easily it comes to you.
(Plus: Check out our Habit Workshop course.)

1. **Just do it** – Don't think about it too much. It is possible to emotionally declutter, so just do it!
2. **Find your muse** – Think of someone you know who is very good at overcoming emotional difficulty. What would they do? How would they do it? Copy and repeat.
3. **Visions of greatness** – Think of a clear-minded, emotionally-free person who inspires you. Bring his/her image to your mind.
4. **Imagine people cheering for you** – A huge imaginary audience, all rooting for *your* emotional decluttering success. That can help you run the extra mile.
5. **Start small** – Pick *one* action related to emotional decluttering and make that your sole goal. If that works you can re-assess.
6. **Start easy** – Begin with what's easiest for you to declutter emotionally and then work your way towards the more complex tasks.
7. **Ignore voices of failure** – Hearing voices again? The ones that halt your emotional decluttering in its tracks? Don't let those voices (telling you that you can't succeed) win. Send them on vacation for a week.
8. **Focus on past success** – Think of a time you were successful at pushing yourself in the past – what worked for you then? How can you recreate that motivation now to emotionally declutter?
9. **Spiritualize it** – Recognize emotional decluttering as a means to a more holistic, spiritual you.
10. **Enlist help** – Sharing your journey with a friend or partner will help get you through the slump.

Add your items to the list:

11. _____

12. _____

13. _____

Which emotions do you want to declutter most?

Rate the following, to help yourself realize which emotions need to be decluttered somewhat or entirely, in order to reach an emotional balance you are comfortable with.

1. Hatred. It feels good, for a moment, but doesn't actually help you achieve anything.
2. Anger. It's a great tool, when it's necessary. If you hold on too long it morphs into pointless revenge and hatred.
3. Grudge. By keeping a grudge you're allowing the person who hurt you control over you and your mind.
4. Envy. It's just tiring, always looking around and desiring what others have.
5. Anxiety. If you're always stressed about everything, you can't be enjoying anything. Nothing is so worrisome that it's worth missing out on life for it.
6. Regret. Regret is only useful if you learn from it, for the future. Regretting something just because it shouldn't have happened is a waste of time. Once you figure out something to learn from your regret, you'll find the regret itself lessens.
7. Inadequacy. Either you can or you can't. If you can, great. If you can't, also great: find what it is you can do. Everyone's good at something, and it's a shame to walk through life feeling inadequate just because you haven't found what's right for you.

How writing a to-do list was half the decluttering battle

If God is in the details, then apparently her angels are in to-do lists. I couldn't believe how manageable tasks became once they were on a to-do list that I could tackle. Did you have a similar experience? Share it with the community! Spend five minutes writing about such an experience you've had recently in your 'Declutter Your Mind ' journal.

Direct message us YOUR story @Buddy_N_Soul on Instagram and be anonymously featured for a chance to **win a Buddy&Soul three month free membership**.

I need to declutter my home before I declutter my mind!

How can my mind ever be clear when I live in such a wreck?

For:

1. If I can't find the time to clear my house of all the junk I have, there's no way I'm going to find time to work on something as abstract as decluttering my mind.
2. Not just my living room!! My life is too hectic as it is, I wouldn't know where to start.
3. What's the point of decluttering my mind if I come home to a house full of junk every day?
4. My cluttered house, cluttered schedule and cluttered PTA meetings are what are weighing on my mind!

Add you own argument:

5. _____

Against:

1. One has nothing to do with the other. It makes no difference which you declutter first.
2. You gotta start somewhere – decluttering you mind will probably make you find the wherewithal to declutter your living room.
3. Truth be told, since decluttering my mind can be done anywhere and anytime, I could probably find the time to do this before I find the time to declutter my living room.
4. You know what? Let's just start and see if I can do this. There's nothing to lose.

Add you own argument:

5. _____

STRATEGY 4: Banish stress

Last session we tackled some of our practical to-dos, but beneath our mental stack of sticky notes, we tend to carry a second pile – a hidden pile – containing all the items that we find terrifying, maybe shameful, or otherwise desperately want to avoid.

Not only does this type of emotional clutter take up precious mental energy, but it can even operate on a physiological level, sending destructive stress signals through our bodies when we least want or need them. Being stressed about things we aren't doing, things we can't control, and things we can't change takes our attention away from what we want to be doing. It inhibits us from accomplishing tasks easily possible with just a little more focus. Getting some of these things off our mind will both free us from the background preoccupation and make us available to tackle more important things.

(Plus: Check out our Stress Management course.)

Allow me to indulge in another personal story: I used to work as a teacher. Before I started studying for my teaching degree, I dreaded the practice teaching placements I knew I'd have to complete as requirements for the program. I started losing sleep about them before the school year even began, having nightmares about being assigned to a monster host teacher, being trampled by an unruly class, and becoming the laughing stock of the whole school. Needless to say, I was stressed.

Well, finally that first placement did roll around and guess what...it was fine! It was even surprisingly enjoyable, and, while I might not have been the star of the staff room, I certainly was no laughing stock.

After a few short weeks, when it was all over, I looked back and laughed at the anxiety I had created for myself for no reason at all. I had built up an ogre in my imagination and fed it my fears, stress, and negative thoughts until it grew so large that I was paralyzed.

These days I recognize that fear of the unknown can be a major anxiety trigger for me and I try to stop it in its tracks before it gets out of control. I recognize it for what it is and make a conscious decision that it won't stop me from pursuing my goals. Fear is part of life, I tell myself. Real life is messy. And that's okay. I harness the fear as motivation to pursue and accomplish my larger goals. **A sense of pressure can be useful if it motivates me to action, but that toxic type of stress is never good – not for the body, mind, or soul.**

What I have also learned is to harness the power of visualization to my benefit. According to Shakti Gawain, best-selling author and pioneer in the field of personal development, visualization is a powerful tool for banishing unnecessary stress in our lives. In her book, *Creative Visualization: Use the Power of Your Imagination to Create What You Want in Your Life,* Gawain writes that visualization is "about learning to use your natural creative imagination in a more and more conscious way." Rather than let your mind run wild, "the use of creative visualization gives us a key to tap into the natural goodness and bounty of life" (p. 4). Instead of visualizing a worst-case-scenario and being stressed out by it, we can visualize a really good outcome. This will hopefully encourage us to pursue the opportunity.

I know personally that this not only soothes me, but also teaches me what this positive process and outcome could look like. If I follow this dream scenario, it might actually come to fruition.

DRIVING THE MESSAGE HOME

Hello again, today we've got The Minimalists with their take on mental clutter.

Joshua Fields Millburn & Ryan Nicodemus discuss the American consumer mindset and relate it to internal clutter. They also address some of their most frequently-asked questions, like 'is there a connection between physical clutter and mental clutter?' And 'What is the best way to declutter your mind?' In terms of material possessions, Joshua says "everything I own adds real value to my life…everything I own serves a purpose or brings me joy." This directly translates to the effects of ridding your mind of mental clutter and embracing those things that truly add value to your life, and let you find a sense of inner peace.

Watch 'The Art of Letting Go' presented by The Minimalists at TEDxFargo on YouTube.

EXERCISE

Think of any upcoming events or obligations that are occupying too much precious real estate in your mind, causing you to be stressed: e.g. a dreaded visit to the dentist, a work trip out of town, and a conversation with your mother-in-law. Think about those dreaded-stress-inducing responsibilities that are looming and for which you cannot see an easy fix. Now choose one and write it down in your journal.

Next, close your eyes and imagine your most dreaded event playing out in a surprisingly harmless way. In fact, you can envision the best-case scenario. Watch yourself work through a stressful challenge or successfully fulfil an annoying obligation and see how proud you feel. In your journal, write out the best-case scenario that you envisioned. Be sure to include how it makes you feel when you believe that this is possible.

TIPS

Tip 1: You have nothing to gain by living and envisioning the worst-case scenario. If there's nothing you can do about it anyway, why not at least envision a hopeful outcome?

Tip 2: If you enjoyed using your mind in a different way by visualizing new alternatives, be sure to check out our Everyday Reframing course and see how far you can take it.

6 signs You're too stressed about being stress-free

Are you always being told to let go of the stress? Just shouted at to be stress free already? Well, here are some signs that you, like me, are getting too stressed about the carelessness of it all! (Plus: Check out our Stress Management course.)

1. Whenever I do anything, I get locked into circuitous thoughts of whether it will make me more stressed, or more-calm, and why.
2. When I am engaged in "calming" activities, I can't stop checking my watch every couple of minutes.
3. I've started feeling grateful for objectively stressful situations, because I don't have to explain myself to anyone over them!

Add your items to the list:

4. _____

5. _____

6. _____

13 ways decluttering your mind will reduce stress

Do you have those pesky worries that are just sitting there, chilling in the back of your mind? These are 10 stress relievers, courtesy of decluttering.
(Plus: Check out our Stress Management course.)

1. Accepting yourself can minimize the stressful gap between who you are and who you "ought to be."
2. Relinquishing control helps you live in the present moment, not worrying about the past or future. Decluttering your mind has a lot to do with relinquishing control, realizing that some things just aren't in your hands, and letting them go.
3. Recognizing your limitations helps you set realistic and attainable goals, not unattainable frustrating ones.
   (Plus: Check out our Achieve Your Goals course.)
4. Re-assessing your life helps you identify and start to eliminate or reduce recurrent stressors.
5. Tying up your loose ends – all those "when I get around to its" – helps you stop the cycle of accumulating mental clutter. From now on, you can deal with things as they arise.
6. Quieting the negative voices of your past empowers you to move beyond.
7. You can focus on that which can be changed and accept that which cannot.
8. A clear mind enables you to distinguish between *actual* stress and *imagined* stress – that which you build up in your own mind.
9. It gives you coping tools to deal with stressors that do arise.
10. Surrounding yourself with positive and supportive people can turn your life around in the best way!

Add your items to the list:

11. _____

12. _____

13. _____

How I imagined my way out of being stressed

Many of us were quick to check our imaginations at the door of adulthood. And yet, imagination can play a profound and healing role, especially when it comes to stress and mental clutter. Share your experiences with the community, and help others who are facing similar challenges. Spend five minutes writing about such an experience you've had recently in your 'Declutter Your Mind' journal.

Direct message us YOUR story @Buddy_N_Soul on Instagram and be anonymously featured for a chance to **win a Buddy&Soul three month free membership**.

9 situations where I struggle to declutter my mind

I want to learn how to find inner peace as much as the next person, but sometimes I struggle. There are limits, and here are mine.

1. Just like anything else - I have to feel that I chose this on my own.
2. When I have waaaaay too much going on in there, and I feel overwhelmed with life as it is. The thought of where to even start is scary.
3. I am going through a transitional period in my life – a break-up, a move, a new job, a new kid – for me, the timing here just ain't gonna work. To find inner peace you first need some outer-peace.
4. When there's no one I can talk to about it. I need some support!
5. When I feel like I am great and perfect and my life needs no improvement.
6. I feel a little fruity telling people I'm searching for inner peace, or a clear mind. It sounds too new-agey, and I guess I'm too cynical.

Add your items to the list:

7. _____

8. _____

9. _____

STRATEGY 5: Close your expectation gap

At this point in the course, you're ready to take the plunge and delve into some of the deeper issues that clutter your mind. This starts with taking an honest look at how you're living your life and closing your expectation gaps.

Here's what that means.

Some people live life in two parallel universes: In Universe 1, they're with the family they've got, the car they drive, and the job they work, all of which can be very nice. Then, in Universe 2, they're where they think they need to be – whom they think they need to be married to, what their kids should be doing, what car they should be driving, and so forth. This is essentially comparing the real with the ideal.

If there's a gap between where you are in life and how you feel about this place, your mind may be cluttered with various regrets and disappointed musings. Now is the time to explore it and maybe patch things up between who you are and who you thought you'd be, and find inner peace where you are.

Not all of us can win MasterChef, or go on to become the CEO of a Fortune 500 company.

Not all of us can be law firm partners, billing over $1,000 an hour. However, not all law firm partners billing over $1,000 an hour are happy.

Not all of us who thought we'd raise five or six kids end up doing so.

And not all of us who dreamed of having a royal wedding end up with prince (or princess) charming.

So what? Sometimes these things are fun to dream about, but they are not really meant to be achieved.

By all means, dream big, but when dreams turn from fantasies into *expectations*, they quickly lose their charm and end up costing you your inner peace. Instead of a source of inspiration, they become a source of despair – despair that you are not where you think you should be. These "dreams" are dangerous mirrors, making your life look pale and meaningless by comparison to where you imagine you ought to be. Christine Hassler, a former Hollywood agent who left her job in order to pursue a life of passion, calls this gap an "expectation hangover." In her book *Expectation Hangover: Free Yourself from Your Past, Change Your Present and Get What You Really Want*, she writes that "the cure to Expectation Hangovers is *not* to figure out another way to get what we thought we wanted, but rather to move out of our own way enough to see what we really need" (p.6).

This exercise right here is the mother of honest. It means looking at yourself for who you are and who you're not, what you have accomplished and what you probably won't and coming to terms with it. Hard? Maybe; but not as hard as living with constant comparisons to what you "*should*" be accomplishing, always chasing inner peace while you're pushing it away.

So take a look at what you've got. Own it. Love it. And here is how.

DRIVING THE MESSAGE HOME

Thank you for joining us for the next session. We know you have what it takes – now prove it to yourself. Let's say you thought you'd be on route A in life and you've been on route B via C and D… Ever wonder what it's like to live with no regrets and walk through life uncluttered by them? Watch Lizzie Velazquez's talk about defining yourself, and gain the confidence you need to be on a different path than the one you planned for. Lizzie is inspiring and motivating; even though things are hard for her, she doesn't let it define her.

Watch 'How Do You Define Yourself?' presented by Lizzie Velasquez at TEDxAustinWomen on YouTube.

EXERCISE

Imagine a night train, where you sit next to a stranger. You begin confessing all the things you always wanted to achieve, and never got around to. **You confess your regrets and things you wish you could have done earlier in life.** Whether they are big or small, professional or personal, spill it all out. List them all in your journal, and underneath them, write: **AND THAT'S OKAY!**

TIPS

Tip 1: While it may sting to see all the things you haven't done, remember that you're actually saying goodbye to regrets that are getting in your way.

Tip 2: If you just can't let go of an item on your list, check out our Priorities Reboot course, and figure out whether it's truly mental clutter, or a goal you really want to achieve!

Tip 3: For more on differentiating between who you are and whom you feel you ought to be, check out our courses Defining Your Identity and Cultivating Authenticity.

Tip 4: Check out our Achieve Your Goals course to gain more direction on setting a realistic, achievable direction for your life.

Letting go of where I "should" be means I'm a loser!

There's a reason I've been keeping track of where I "should" be! Why should I let that go, and with it hopes of ever getting there?

For:

1. Where I "should" be gives me hope. Getting rid of it means accepting that I'm a loser for life.
2. Getting rid of ambition? Isn't that a bit defeatist?
3. Where I should be is an honest estimate of my life. If I fall short, it's only my fault.

Add you own argument:

4. _____

Against:

1. "Should" is in the past. You can't have hope about the past. By all means, hang on to where you *want* to be, and work towards it!
2. "Should" isn't ambition, it's reprimand. That's what's defeatist, because you'll never be able to achieve it!
3. Honestly, there's no such thing as "should". If it didn't happen, there's no saying that it should have.

Add you own argument:

4. _____

6 personality traits that will help you to emotionally declutter negative thoughts

A mental declutter is always difficult, but if you have these traits, they might just help you out a bit more than you might have thought.

1. Introversion. Because you enjoy spending time with your number one person--- you—it won't be difficult to introspect on what you need to get rid of and what can stay.
2. Achievement seeker. While it may frustrate you to try something you're not naturally good at, your immense drive to succeed can help ensure you'll stick at it until you do!
3. Self-assuredness. When you decide to do something, you aren't eaten by doubts. Your stout belief that this is right for you might be the most important tool you have for success!

Add your items to the list:

4. _____

5. _____

6. _____

I never dreamed having more mental energy could lead to this

Decluttering your mind sounds like a nice idea, perhaps, but it's one of those things you can't really anticipate. There's no telling how it's going to feel for each individual. How did it feel for you? What were some of the surprising consequences of decluttering your mind? Share with the community, below. Spend five minutes writing about such an experience you've had recently in your 'Declutter Your Mind' journal.

Direct message us YOUR story @Buddy_N_Soul on Instagram and be anonymously featured for a chance to **win a Buddy&Soul three month free membership**.

How I learned to let go of goals that made no sense

Everyone has goals they want to achieve, and goals that they like to think about. What's hard is knowing the difference, and realizing when you need to stop pursuing goals that don't really make sense, and stop feeling bad about not achieving them. Share how you were able to make that distinction, and let go of goals that really made no sense. Spend five minutes writing about such an experience you've had recently in your 'Declutter Your Mind' journal.

Direct message us YOUR story @Buddy_N_Soul on Instagram and be anonymously featured for a chance to **win a Buddy&Soul three month free membership**.

STRATEGY 6: Declutter people in your life

"Keep away from people who belittle your ambitions. Small people always do that, but the really great make you feel that you, too, can become great." – Mark Twain

Decluttering people is a big job. It can sometimes take years of therapy to come to the realization that someone close to us has got to go. But alongside that, there are also those friends who, where our emotional connection to them is concerned, already have one foot out the door. Friends we don't really care about anymore but we keep up with out of inertia.

Ditto for communities and social groups that are a part of the past and not the future. I remember when I moved cities, I couldn't bring myself to leave my former community's Facebook group; I wasn't ready to let go, and I wanted to know what my former friends were up to. The problem? My inbox was so full of what my past community was doing that I spent a lot of time wallowing in what I was missing out on and couldn't focus on what I could be gaining by focusing on and actively participating in my present community.

As for friends, weeding them out may sound cruel, but sometimes it is necessary. A friend is someone you enjoy being with, someone who cares about you, and whose advice is given with your best interest in mind. Definitely not someone who puts you down or is otherwise toxic. Are you putting up with them just because it's what you're used to? Or perhaps you just never quite figured out how out to say goodbye. Maybe it did not even occur to you that you could live without them…

There seldom comes a moment when we ask ourselves these questions, but we should. Because choices we make about whom we surround ourselves with and whose advice we take to heart can have a strong impact on how we live our life and the decisions we make.

When someone really hurt me, driving me to question my own judgment and feel incapacitated, my friend Alice pointed to my head and said, "If someone wants to play here, they have to play nice." We don't want people spreading mean thoughts about the world or worse, about ourselves.

And we're not only talking about extremes. Even if you a friend who isn't toxic but causes you to feel a bit empty or uncomfortable inside, consider whether it's a friendship you're still interested in maintaining. Sometimes, we unwittingly deprive ourselves of the opportunity to be with people we truly care for, or who bring higher value to our life, simply because we never really thought about it.
Now's the time to change that. Now's the time to make conscious choices about the people you let into your life.

DRIVING THE MESSAGE HOME

Hello again, the next bit is going to require some brutal honesty and confidence. You can do this. Nobody can make you feel inferior without your consent. In this video, Koi Fresco, the YouTube personality who posts content, covering everything from science to philosophy, discusses toxic relationships and how to get out of them. Let this clip help you figure out if you're in a toxic relationship and if so, how to deal with it. You don't need that kind of negativity in your life and if you can't declutter them, figure out how to make yourself stronger so it doesn't affect you at all!

Watch 'Toxic Relationships! Why We Stay & How to Leave' presented by Koi Fresco on YouTube.

EXERCISE

Step 1: Identify a questionable "friend" you're holding onto and take the following survey:

1. Can I be myself around this person?
2. Do we have quality conversations on topics I am comfortable with?
3. Does he or she take me down paths I want to go?
4. Do I feel good about myself after being with this friend?
5. Do I look forward to seeing him or her?

Scoring: (1-never, 2-occasionally, 3-some of the time, 4-often, 5-always)

Total score of 5-10 – You scored ____. This suggests that your "friendship" might be causing more harm than good. Consider making changes in the relationships or parting ways.

11-15 – You scored ____. This suggests that your friendship may be beneficial in some ways and harmful in others. Consider how much you are willing to invest in the relationship and make a change.

16-20 – You scored ____. This suggests that your friendship is for the most part beneficial. Consider how you can change the things that aren't working with the friendship.

21-25 – You scored ____. This suggests that your friendship is having a good influence on you. It's a keeper!

Step 2: Did the questionnaire give you any new insights into your friendship with this person? What steps will you take to either improve your relationship or to actively put up the proper boundaries?

TIPS

Tip 1: If you are feeling guilty about "decluttering" people in your life, think of this as 're-allocating your time, so you can spend more of it in healthier relationships'. You only have so much time – why spend it with people who aren't good for you? For more on how to reconcile such issues, check out our Everyday Reframing course.

Tip 2. Decluttering a friend does not need to be a dramatic process; you can let them slide away by unfollowing their Facebook feed, for example, so you notice them less. Over time, the negative noise isn't present in your life. It doesn't have to be overtly noticeable or uncomfortable.

Tip 3: Does this feel strange? Maybe it's because you're used to being with this person. Think of this as rehab – difficult in the short run, but worth it in the long run.

Tip 4: If you know this is the right thing to do but are concerned over hurting your "friend's" feelings, we are here to remind you that your first obligation is to take good care of yourself.

Motivations to declutter difficult friends

You've been convinced that it's important to declutter difficult friends, but when it gets right down to it, he saw you through a tough time, and she was there when you were in a tight spot. Here are some motivational boosts to help you declutter difficult friends.

1. You wouldn't be considering it if this friend didn't make you feel bad about yourself and your life-decisions.
2. A true friend wouldn't be a candidate for decluttering. If they're up on the block, they've done something to earn it. Remind yourself of this.
3. This isn't forever. A friend you "declutter" today might become close to you again after a cool-down period. Let these things happen non-dramatically and organically, and they'll be reversible.

Did we miss anything? Add it in your journal: _____

What caused you to "declutter" a friend?

This person probably had it coming, but what made you realize they had no place in your life?

1. A mean or thoughtless comment.
2. Never showing willingness to listen to you.
3. Feeling left out even when you organized a meeting.
4. Spending hours after every get-together imagining what you should have said.
5. The realization that they only took from you, but never gave anything positive (even a good feeling).

How decluttering my friends made me less stressed

Stopping to notice who in your life is actually good for you, and who is quietly harming you can be tough. But when you finally realize which friends need to be decluttered, it can greatly ease your stress load. Share with the community how decluttering taught you something about your real friendships. Spend five minutes writing about such an experience you've had recently in your 'Declutter Your Mind' journal.

Direct message us YOUR story @Buddy_N_Soul on Instagram and be anonymously featured for a chance to **win a Buddy&Soul three month free membership**.

6 ways to neutralize negativity in a toxic relationship

It can be easy to identify your toxic friends, but now what? These people have been a part of your life for so long, that it can be hard to just declutter them in a sweep. Here are some tips about how to neutralize their negative effect on you.

1. Unfollow their Facebook, Twitter, or Instagram feeds. You can still look them up if you want to, but becoming less involved in their lives will help you disengage from their negativity.
2. Don't make plans with them. For people who you have to see, make sure to go only to the bare-necessary events (just to meet grandma, but not to dinner afterwards).
3. Think of ways, in advance, to neutralize some of their meaner comments. You know what they're prone to say, now figure out what you'd like to say back to them!

Add your items to the list:

4. _____

5. _____

6. _____

STRATEGY 7: Declutter your false beliefs

We all hold certain assumptions and beliefs about ourselves and the world around us. Often these are both negative and false. And yet, we still operate upon them. Good examples are "I have two left hands," "The good ones are already taken," "My sister is the smart one", "When things are difficult, you might as well quit," etc. Whether these come from our own perceptions and life experiences or from internalizing messages that others (parents, teachers, "friends," ex-partners, etc.) have sent us, these disempowering mantras block us from making progress and achieving what we want in life, and end up using a lot of mental energy that would be better spent elsewhere.

Just like we declutter our wardrobe, weeding out garments which no longer fit or no longer serve us, it's time to declutter and re-examine the premises and assumptions we have about life. Keep the ones that are good for you and get rid of the rest. It's a shame to walk around with the weight of false beliefs. It's a weight you should never have to carry, and it's often heavy enough to squash any hope of finding inner peace.

If you think you have two left hands and avoid doing the simplest things because of it, such as putting together a cordless phone, you are limiting your ability to function in the world. And if you shy from dating, thinking that all the good ones are taken, you might be missing out on a great opportunity to meet and build a relationship with an awesome partner.

(Plus: Check out our Defining your Identity course.)

In the words of self-development author Brian Tracy, "if you believe yourself to be limited in some way, whether or not it is true, it becomes true for you" (*Goals!*, p. 42).

So let's get started on getting rid of those negative thoughts and mantras.
A helpful framework for questioning beliefs comes from leading author and self-inquiry teacher Byron Katie. In her method of self-inquiry which she calls "The Work," Katie puts forth four crucial questions which you can ask yourself about any belief you're holding:
1. Is it true?
2. Can you absolutely know that it's true?
3. How do you react, what happens, when you believe that thought?
4. Who would you be without the thought?

A word of warning: decluttering your false beliefs may be harder than you think, but not too hard for us to suggest it. It requires acknowledging that your beliefs may not be true and coming to terms with the price you've already paid for holding this faith. It does pay off, I promise.

DRIVING THE MESSAGE HOME

Sometimes we don't even realize all the false messages we are storing and how they are impacting our daily lives. Neuroanatomist Jill Bolte Taylor knew intellectually how impactful false beliefs were, but it wasn't until she had a stroke that she was able to understand experientially what life looks like without any previous memories or messages. She describes in amusing detail the morning of the stroke and the freedom of "losing 37 years of emotional baggage". Can you imagine, even momentarily what your life would look like if you could lose a lifetime of your own false beliefs and emotional baggage?

Watch 'My Stroke of Insight' presented by Jill Bolte Taylor on YouTube.

EXERCISE

Step 1: **Close your eyes and let a limiting belief you hold come to the surface. Write it down in your journal.**

Step 2: **Put your limiting belief to the test** using Byron Katie's 4 prompts.

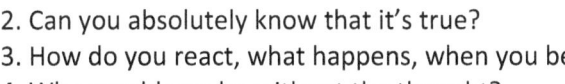

Write down your response to each:

1. Is it true?
2. Can you absolutely know that it's true?
3. How do you react, what happens, when you believe that thought?
4. Who would you be without the thought?

TIPS

Tip 1: Ridding yourself of false beliefs doesn't happen overnight. Be forgiving, but persistent.

Tip 2: You might be feeling overwhelmed by the price you already paid when you followed this false belief. Let bygones be bygones. You cannot change the past, but you can minimize this price going forward and make sure not to make the same mistake twice.

Tip 3: Another way to get rid of assumptions and false beliefs is by reframing them. Instead of "I have two left hands", you could view yourself more favorably, saying "I may not be a master carpenter, but there are many things I'm capable of doing with my hands." Check out our Everyday Reframing course for more.

7 ways for disorganized folk to declutter false beliefs

False beliefs can strike anyone, regardless of organization level. But here are a few tricks for the particularly disorganized to declutter false beliefs.

1. Don't believe everything you hear!
2. I don't care about empirical data but talking to friends I trust and getting their opinions is a great way to challenge my beliefs.
3. Reading about others who have succeeded is a great way to sneak in a decluttering of false beliefs.
4. Hiding reminder-notes to myself. I forget where they are and am always surprised when I find one!

Add your items to the list:

5. _____

6. _____

7. _____

What are your greatest barriers at decluttering false beliefs?

Everyone has them, but somehow, that doesn't help with getting rid of them. What are some of the things that hold you back from decluttering false beliefs?

1. But... I can't get rid of that pestering 'but' thought that follows.
2. The belief is reinforced by my environment. Maybe it's not so false after all?
3. I keep making up excuses, I don't know why. There's always something.
4. It would require too many changes to challenge the belief.
5. I don't have the money to challenge my beliefs.

Add your own:

6. _____

7. _____

8. _____

When I finally confronted my false belief and defeated it

Regardless of how big it is, confronting a false belief is incredibly hard. It requires you to look deeply and honestly into yourself, and change something fundamental about how you think. What was your false belief, and how did you defeat it? Share your story with the community, and read how others are facing similar challenges. Spend five minutes writing about such an experience you've had recently in your 'Declutter Your Mind' journal.

Direct message us YOUR story @Buddy_N_Soul on Instagram and be anonymously featured for a chance to **win a Buddy&Soul three month free membership**.

Success and failure have nothing to do with low mental energy

There are plenty of highly successful people out there with very cluttered minds. I'm a multi-tasker, my mom is a multi-tasker and so is my best friend- why do I need to declutter if I succeed at it?

For:

1. My spouse and my boss (and most everyone around me) can do a gazillion things at once, so there's no reason I shouldn't be able to.
2. Just because I'm thinking of things from the past, doesn't mean I won't be successful. If I'm good at what I do, what does it matter what's going on inside my mind?
3. I don't have the time to try to fool around with changing my mind and my way of thought. I am where I am, there's no way to change it.

Add you own argument:

4. _____

Against:

1. Are you sure what you have now is success?
2. If you think you're succeeding now, just imagine what it could be like if your mind was clear!
3. You've got nothing to lose. If you declutter you may surprise yourself.

Add you own argument:

4. _____

STRATEGY 8: Make amends with the past

"View your life with kindsight. Stop beating yourself up about things from your past. Instead of slapping your forehead and asking, 'What was I thinking,' breathe and ask yourself the kinder question, 'What was I learning?'" – Karen Salmansohn, *The Bounce Back Book: How to Thrive in the Face of Adversity, Setbacks, and Losses.*

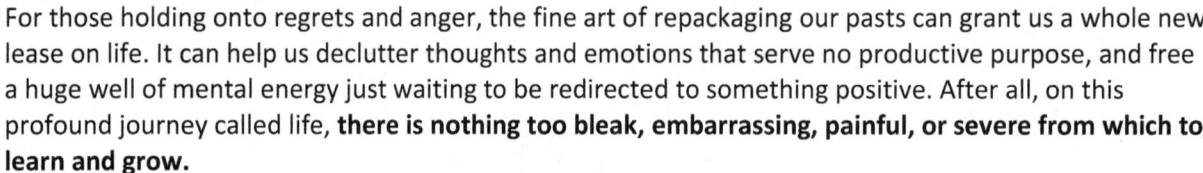

Looking back on your past, what do you see? Do you see a dispersed stream of memories, random events, some good, some glorious, some bad, some ugly – or do you see a gentle thread weaving all these seeming disparate moments together, ultimately leading you to who, what, and where you are today?

For those holding onto regrets and anger, the fine art of repackaging our pasts can grant us a whole new lease on life. It can help us declutter thoughts and emotions that serve no productive purpose, and free a huge well of mental energy just waiting to be redirected to something positive. After all, on this profound journey called life, **there is nothing too bleak, embarrassing, painful, or severe from which to learn and grow.**

Consider the words of Byron Katie in reference to her development of "The Work" – the self-inquiry process we practiced last session: "The Work reveals that what you think shouldn't have happened should have happened. It should have happened because it did, and no thinking in the world can change it" (*Loving What Is*, p.2.).

She goes on to explain that no one wishes disaster upon themselves, but that when undesirable events do happen, "how can it be helpful to mentally argue with them?" (p.2.). We know we shouldn't, and yet we do. We use mental energy to argue with reality, dwell on our predicament, and turn away, towards our regrets and towards those actions that, no matter how hard we try, we just cannot change.

What we can change, however, is where we turn our gaze, and how much time we spend looking in each direction, before we choose to look ahead.

(Plus: Check out our Tackling Change course.)

DRIVING THE MESSAGE HOME

Greetings! We are very happy to see you here today. Onwards and upwards. We are on our way to decluttering our minds. Today, we focus on regrets, and that's an amazing thing. Dealing with our regrets has the potential to help clear out huge areas of our brain! However, it's certainly not an easy process. It can sometimes feel like decluttering regrets means not caring that bad things happened, or sweeping all of your negative emotions under the rug and hoping no one notices the lump.

Making peace with regrets doesn't mean ignoring them. Listen to Kathryn Schulz discuss her biggest regret, and how she learned to move forward from it. Not by deciding it didn't matter, but by deciding it did.

Watch 'Don't Regret Regret' presented by Kathryn Schulz on YouTube.

EXERCISE

Identify a memory of one of your less glorious moments. Ask yourself: In retrospect, **what can or did you learn from the experience?** Use your journal to write freely any reactions that come to mind. Let the positive lessons sink in.

TIPS

Tip 1: Note that this does not erase the negative memory, nor taint it a false, brash pink. It just helps you come to terms with it, learn the lesson and move on. Try it again with a new memory.

Tip 2: Regrets and pent up anger will inevitably create stress. If this exercise makes you realize this is an issue for you, try our Stress Management course.

7 ways to say goodbye to the pain of regret

Regret seems like it's there for a reason, but more often than not it only holds us back. Here are some ways to let go of the pain of regrets, without sugarcoating the past or our mistakes.

1. I remind myself that it happened and it's done, and worrying about it will not change it.
2. Whenever I find myself worrying at my regret, I repeat to myself what I learned from it. After a while, I jump straight to the lesson, without thinking about the regret.
3. I tell myself that the "me" back then needed this mistake, for some reason. No point in being angry at past-me, for what those needs were back then.
4. I try to learn from my mistakes and my regrets. It may be unavoidable the first time, but don't let it happen to you twice.

Add your items to the list:

5. _____

6. _____

7. _____

How dealing with regrets allowed me to focus

Everyone has regrets and roads-not-taken. It's how you deal with them that can either make you eternally preoccupied with "what if," or help set you on a new road. Share with the community how your dealt with your regrets, and what it taught you about yourself, moving forward. Spend five minutes writing about such an experience you've had recently in your 'Declutter Your Mind' journal.

Direct message us YOUR story @Buddy_N_Soul on Instagram and be anonymously featured for a chance to **win a Buddy&Soul three month free membership**.

What I learned from my bad experience

Everyone finds a slightly different way to deal with negative experiences from their past. Some learn lessons, some are able to appreciate how the experience was key in ultimately moving them forward, and some are able to just let it go. What did you learn from your bad experience? Share your conclusions with the community, and maybe inspire others to try your unique way of letting the past go. Spend five minutes writing about such an experience you've had recently in your 'Declutter Your Mind' journal.

Direct message us YOUR story @Buddy_N_Soul on Instagram and be anonymously featured for a chance to **win a Buddy&Soul three month free membership**.

Find inner peace? There's no point – it's fleeting at best.

Your mind is clear, your heart is open, but now your mother-in-aw is in town and your kids are making a mess and you remembered you owe your friend 20 bucks. Is there ever an end to decluttering?

For:

1. That's probably true. It would be pretty annoying to discover in a few weeks that you're right back to square one.
2. The only things worth investing in are those that are permanent. And with emotions, there's never a guarantee.
3. I know I'll feel like a failure if it doesn't last. Then I'll have to go and "declutter" my feelings of being a failure; and then my feelings on those feelings and then... *ad infinitum*.

Add you own argument:

4. _____

Against:

1. Emotional decluttering might last longer than you think (assuming you're not a prophet).
2. Doing a major emotional declutter could start you on a whole new path and way of living, where you accrue much less 'clutter' as you go along.
3. Even if it doesn't last completely, a light "follow-up cleaning" will be much less painstaking and time-consuming.
4. Once you've pushed yourself to do a major emotional declutter once, you're likely to actually *want* to do it a second time (if needed) because you remember how good it felt.

Add you own argument:

5. _____

STRATEGY 9: Declutter "floater moments"

How you spend your time means more than which activities you fill it with. It has to do with *what's going on in your mind* as time moves moment by moment and you go about your daily activities. Let's now focus on the positive things we need and want to fill our minds.

Every single day grants us a string of moments that we can choose to seize or let slide by. When we just go with the flow and drift on auto-pilot, we empower our mental and emotional clutter to creep in and hinder our focus. These undirected pockets of time, or "floater moments," open us up to things like rumination, stress, and all those negative thought patterns we've been working so hard to uproot. On the flipside, when we use these moments purposefully, we draw closer to our ultimate goals, generating a greater sense of clarity, calm, and peace of mind. And isn't that why we came here in the first place?

In *The Ecstasy of Surrender: 12 Surprising Ways Letting Go Can Empower Your Life* (2014), author and psychologist Dr. Judith Orloff speaks about how she stays intentional about her goals no matter where she is or what she's doing. Orloff says, "I seek happiness wherever I go. Whether I'm presenting a keynote address or waiting in line at the post office, it's in the doing that the ecstasy comes" (p. 5). While Orloff is speaking specifically about her goal of happiness, you could replace that with any goal that brought you to this course. How do you fill those pockets of time when *you're* waiting in line at the post office? Where does your mind go?

One way to refocus your "floater moments" is to introduce a specific practice, like mindfulness or gratitude, to replace your automatic thoughts.

According to Jon Kabat-Zinn, founder of Mindfulness Based Stress Reduction Therapy (MBSR), "A diminished awareness of the present moment inevitably creates other problems for us as well through our unconscious and automatic actions and behaviors, often driven by deep seated fears and insecurities" (*Wherever You Go, There You Are: Mindfulness Meditation in Everyday Life,* p. 4). His solution? Mindfulness. In Kabat-Zinn's words, "Mindfulness provides a simple but powerful route for getting ourselves unstuck, back into touch with our own wisdom and vitality" (p. 5). Being mindful, or more simply put, paying attention, can prevent the automatic thoughts from taking the driver's seat.

Practicing gratitude is another powerful option. Instead of rushing to check your phone, use "floater moments" to run through everything you're grateful for at that moment.

Let's make good use of pockets of time by fine-tuning our thoughts and mental orientation, seizing opportunities we never even knew existed to create a meaningful life.

DRIVING THE MESSAGE HOME

Welcome! We certainly love each moment you spend with us. Author Mitch Albom should know about looking for pockets of time and making each moment matter; he is the author of the bestselling book *Tuesdays with Morrie* where he went from a busy "no time for anything" journalist to making time for his elderly dying professor. Morrie didn't give lessons for dying; he gave Mitch invaluable life lesson for living the decluttered simple life of love and happiness.

Listen to Mitch inspire you with Morrie, the quiet gentle teacher of mankind who knew how to listen, maximize his time, prioritize and loved to teach others how to make the best of their lives.

(Plus: Check out our Priorities Reboot and Achieve Your Goals courses.)

EXERCISE

Step 1: **Identify a pocket of time during your day or week that you usually spend mentally floating**, like waiting in line at the supermarket, exercising, or driving carpool. Write it down in your journal and commit to making it a mindful moment next time you find yourself there!

Step 2: Right now, practice bringing purpose and intention to your present moment by **simply being grateful for one full minute.** Focus your thoughts on everything you are grateful for at this very moment. When you're done, list everything you thought of in your journal. See how productive one minute can be?

TIPS

Tip 1: You can choose what 'paying attention' means. It can either mean tuning into your surroundings – the sights, sounds, and smells all around you – or noticing what's going on inside of yourself – how does your body feel? Where do your thoughts go when you're not guiding them?

Tip 2: For more on paying attention to the present, check out our Mindfulness for Beginners course.

Things every extrovert should do with a pocket of time

You love the company, the people, the noise. But now you've found yourself in an unexpected pocket of time so... How do you use it?
(Plus: Check out our Mindfulness for Beginners and Priorities Reboot courses.)

1. Tell yourself that it's time to spend some one-on-one with your most awesome friend: you.
2. Thrill-seeking is fantastic! But only if you have the quiet times to compare it with. Otherwise it rather loses its meaning.
3. Taking a minute to slow things down may be against your nature, but really, so is flossing. Doesn't mean it isn't important!

6 things every introvert should do with a pocket of time

You live in pockets of time. You thrive there, in the solitude and introspection. So maybe you're wondering how you could possible make even more of them. Well, here are a few tips:
(Plus: Check out our Mindfulness for Beginners **and** Priorities Reboot **courses.)**

1. Use your natural gift for introspection to watch your thoughts. Note what thoughts arise when you're not trying to control them.
2. Try a visualization technique, like imagining an open window at the back of your mind and allowing each thought to simply drift out of it. Or placing all your "cluttery" thoughts on a TV screen, and then turning off the TV.
3. Pick a thought and stick with it. Introverts are blessed with an unparalleled ability to concentrate. Put your skills to good use by choosing a helpful, soothing topic, and sticking with it for a set amount of time.

Add your items to the list:

4. _____

5. _____

6. _____

I can't control my thoughts— is there any point in trying?

Thoughts by definition are something that happen to you. If someone could control them, there would be no Stream of Consciousness **and no** James Joyce**! So why should I bother trying?**

For:

1. If you don't control your thoughts, they'll control you. It's totally up to you which happens.
2. Thoughts are a habit. You may not be able to control them now, but like any habit, practice makes perfect.
   (Plus: Check out our Habit Workshop course.)
3. Try it out small, and see if you can't. You'll be surprised at how quickly you become adept at it.

Add you own argument:

4. _____

Against:

1. Not only can't I, but I don't want to! My free imagination is who I am!
2. So you mean to say that no one needs to have a negative thought, ever? That it's completely a question of self-control?
3. If I control my thoughts, I'll be quickly reduced to automaton. No thank you!

Add you own argument:

4. _____

The weird pocket of time I used for personal growth

Everyone knows you can read on the bus, or meditate when you have a free hour in your schedule. But what's that weird pocket of time you discovered, and how did you fill it? Share with the community, and maybe help inspire someone to use a pocket of time they hadn't thought of! Spend five minutes writing about such an experience you've had recently in your 'Declutter Your Mind' journal.

Direct message us YOUR story @Buddy_N_Soul on Instagram and be anonymously featured for a chance to **win a Buddy&Soul three month free membership**.

11 ways decluttering your mind helped you

Let's count the ways you come out on top!

1. My 25th college reunion. So many alternative routes presented themselves, but I stuck to my own life, did not compare or feel inferior, and for once, enjoyed it.
2. My in-laws. Say no more.
3. Finally realizing that a "friend" was toxic. And sending her off to be toxic somewhere else.
4. Like going to the gym to stay healthy, it's helped keep me mentally on top.
5. Finally allowing myself to let go of regrets I've been holding to since childhood.
6. It helped me find the real me –and like that person.
7. Stopped comparing myself to my siblings, even though everyone else in my family still does.
8. Empowered me to pursue a new career path and actually admit that I hated my old job, even though it checked all the boxes – as far as everyone else was concerned.

Add your items to the list:

9. _____

10. _____

11. _____

STRATEGY 10: Experience your newfound peace of mind

So, you've gone through your to-dos, your hidden nags, your false beliefs; you've weeded out false expectations of yourself and damaging voices getting in your way... bravo! You are about to enter a new era, and discover a new you. **You will hopefully feel less overwhelmed by life and will experience a plethora of benefits that come along with a clutter-free mind.** Less noise equals more efficiency squared! Just ask Einstein.

After all your hard work, this session is about finally letting yourself *experience* some of the fruits of your labor. But, rather than know this cognitively, we want you to know it experientially.

This involves zoning in on that newfound sense of clarity that you've been working towards. Call it peace, happiness, clarity, calm, Nirvana, Zen – at the end of the day, it's that warm sensation we're all familiar with that eludes definition.

In her book *Finding Your Way in a Wild New World: Reclaim your True Nature to Find the Life you Want*, Dr. Martha Beck refers to this state as a state of "Wordlessness." As she so eloquently phrases it, "Wordlessness allows us to... heal from the violence of a thought system that cuts us apart, destroying our compassion for ourselves and others... it is a blissful and absorbing experience, a place where concepts dissolve and everything is love" (p.8).

So, let's end the course by taking the time to visit that place "where concepts dissolve and everything is love". You certainly deserve this inner peace!

DRIVING THE MESSAGE HOME

You made it to the last session and now let's take our final deep dive.

As we approach the end of the course, it's important to reflect on the process of decluttering. If our goal is to have a clear mind and the sense of inner peace that goes with it, we are finally getting to a stage where we can take a deep breath, and truly reflect on how clear our minds really are. But wordlessness isn't limited only to this one action. Knowing how to feel ourselves, and express ourselves, even without words is a skill that can help us feel more connected to who we are, regardless of where we are and what we're doing. And that's the true secret to decluttering. There will always be one more thing to do, or one more errand to run. But if you can access expression without words, you can clear your mind even if for a moment. Benjamin Zander has made it his life's mission to explain why we all should love classical music. And while this TED Talk won't necessarily change your musical tastes, you might find it helps you rethink what it means to be wordless, and how much depth you can find.

Watch 'Music and Passion' presented by Benjamin Zander on YouTube.

EXERCISE

Step 1: Take a moment right now to **close your eyes, breathe deeply, and enjoy the quiet space you've opened up in your mind.** Note what (if any) words or images come to mind and what that clear space looks like for you.

Step 2: **Upload an image that represents that quiet space** you've been working towards throughout the course. Post your picture on Instagram and Twitter, tagging @Buddy_N_Soul, and Facebook @Buddy&Soul using the hashtag #BuddynSoulWellness. By sharing with us on social media, not only can you help others with their personal journeys, you can read about those facing similar challenges.

TIPS

Tip 1: If you don't know where to begin, you can always focus on your breath. Images will come to mind, explore them.

Tip 2: Experiencing this wordless state doesn't come naturally in our culture, but practice makes perfect. Each time we practice, we build our wordlessness muscles, allowing us to experience it more deeply and access it more readily in the future. The first time always presents the most resistance.

Tip 3: If you loved Declutter your Mind as much as we hope you did, pass it forward!

6 Signs you're amazing at decluttering your mind

It's a long process, but how can you know if you're succeeding?

1. You don't feel any anguish over letting things go.
2. When prompted, you relish the opportunity to get things off your chest, like overdue apologies or thank-you notes!
3. Your brain feels lighter; no longer worrying about all these little things took a weight off your mind!

Add your items to the list:

4. _____

5. _____

6. _____

13 ways to identify a person who is mental-clutter free

You know her; that roommate who skidded in everywhere by the skin of her teeth, so laidback she's horizontal and beautiful inside and out.

1. Shrugs things off. She really doesn't care if things go wrong or if others perceive her negatively.
2. Comfortable in his own skin. He isn't always trying to impress or second guess himself.
3. Able to communicate her emotions clearly and concisely. You don't have to guess where you stand with her: she'll let you know.
4. Doesn't blame. If something goes wrong, he'll try to fix it, rather than waste time pointing fingers.
5. Does what she can to change whatever's changeable and accepts whatever's not. She realizes that it's a waste of energy to worry about things she can't control.
6. Accepts *you* for *you*. He won't try to change you, or to redefine you to suit his needs.
7. Exudes peace and ease. Not in the unbathed hippie way, but in the way that you just know she's not worried about things needlessly.
8. Is generally positive, hopeful, and optimistic. Of course, he might have a bad day, but usually has the frame of mind to wish everyone a sincere good-morning, rather than frowning at his shoes as he rushes past.
9. Is reliable – you can count on her to gets things done. She knows what she can and cannot do, so if she committed to it, you know she has the mental space to deal with it!
10. Is deeply honest. A clutter free person won't bother with lies and deceits, because it's too much wasted energy to keep all the stories straight. He'd rather just be honest, and deal with life as it comes.

Add your items to the list:

11. _____

12. _____

13. _____

My greatest Declutter Your Mind success story

What's your biggest success story with the Declutter Your Mind course? What's the event that happened that made you feel like a decluttering guru? Share your success story with the community! Spend five minutes writing about such an experience you've had recently in your 'Declutter Your Mind' journal.

Direct message us YOUR story @Buddy_N_Soul on Instagram and be anonymously featured for a chance to **win a Buddy&Soul three month free membership**.

13 emotions you could (and *should*) declutter

Everyone experiences all these emotions at one point or another, and that can be a positive thing. But when you let these emotions control you and allow them to grow unchecked, it clutters your mind and holds you back from being... well, you.

1. Hatred. It feels good... for a moment, but it doesn't actually help you achieve anything.
2. Revenge. Vengefulness always promises to be sweet, but you end up dedicating a lot of mental energy to empty fantasies.
3. Anger. It's a great tool, when it's necessary. If you hold on too long it morphs into pointless revenge and hatred.
4. Grudge. By keeping a grudge, you're allowing the person who hurt you control over you and your mind.
5. Fear. Fear, too, is a positive emotion if it keeps you away from a hungry tiger, but fearing things you can't control or predict saps your mental energy faster than you think.
6. Greed. The thing with wanting more, is that there's no limit. There's always one more dollar to be made, or one more argument to win. If you don't cap it, you'll be swallowed whole by it.
7. Envy. It's just tiring, always looking around and desiring what others have.
8. Stress/anxiety. If you're always stressed about everything, you can't be enjoying anything. Nothing is so worrisome that it's worth missing out on life for it.
9. Regret. Regret is only useful if you learn from it, for the future. Regretting something just because it shouldn't have happened is a waste of time. Once you figure out something to learn from your regret, you'll find the regret itself lessens.
10. Inadequacy. Either you can or you can't. If you can, great. If you can't, also great: find what it is you can do. Everyone's good at *something*, and it's a shame to walk through life feeling inadequate just because you haven't found what's right for you. (Plus: Check out our Cultivating Authenticity and Defining your Identity courses.)

Add your items to the list:

11. _____

12. _____

13. _____

WHERE DO WE GO FROM HERE?

You've finished the Declutter Your Mind book, but you haven't finished the journey. It doesn't end, it just gets better. Revisit this book, carry its ideas with you. Check out BuddynSoul.com and the rest of our books for all we have to offer. Spread the word. And change your life for good.

Cultivating Authenticity

Being an authentic person means being true to yourself and knowing *how* to be yourself. It means

making choices that leave you feeling empowered, moving through the world with integrity. It's tough living life with the feeling of, "I don't know who I am," and this course will help you on the road to authenticity by delving into what "being real" means to you, what masks you hide behind and why, and how you can bring to the world all the beauty and joy of who you are and who you want to be.

Goals you can achieve by reading 'Cultivating Authenticity':

- Understand and accept all the parts of who you are, behind your armor.
- Gain tools to live with a greater sense of integrity, inner alignment, and balance.
- Bring to the forefront all the beauty and joy of who you truly are.

Willpower 101

You know what you want to do and where you want to go... You may have accomplished most of it, but you could use some extra oomph. Learn how you can strengthen your willpower by understanding the psychology behind it. You can increase your self-control, helping you stay motivated and on course so you can reach, maintain, and exceed your goals.

Goals you can achieve by reading 'Willpower 101':

- Understand the psychology behind willpower.
- Learn and apply practical tools to help you work towards greater self-control.
- Envision and plan your future successes, with the help of willpower

Stress Management

Feeling stressed, anxious and overwhelmed? Now's the time to take a deep breath and ask yourself how
your stress levels are impacting your life and health. While you might not be able to change your circumstances, this course will help you identify your recurrent stressors and teach you to avoid, work around, or effectively cope with them. The road to calm starts here.

Goals you can achieve by reading 'Stress Management':

- Identify and understand the stressors in your life.
- Learn simple and practical techniques for stress management.
- Create a lasting, less-stressful environment for yourself.

WANT TO LEARN MORE? CHECK THESE OUT!

BOOKS

Broken Open: How Difficult Times Can Help Us Grow by Elizabeth Lesser

Elizabeth Lesser crafts a beautiful blend of moving stories, humorous insights, practical guidance, and personal memoir to give the reader tools to help make the choices and meet challenges head on.

Will we be broken down and defeated or will we use challenge and hardship as impetus for growth? This is the question that perhaps lies at the center of decluttering your mind.

Eat, Pray, Love by Elizabeth Gilbert

A beautifully crafted memoir, Elizabeth Gilbert decides to leave the trappings of American success to find herself. She sets out on a journey to study three different aspects of her nature with three different cultures; Gilbert explores the art of pleasure in Italy, the art of devotion in India, and then a balance between the two on the Indonesian island of Bali.

She realizes that a decluttered mind doesn't mean an empty mind, but how you organize the space.

GADGETS AND OTHER PRODUCTS

Dealing with Guilt - How to find Resolution & Acceptance - DVD

Guilt robs you of joy and energy. Is there a way to move beyond personal imperfections and rise above oppressive remorse? Can guilt ever be constructive?

This program grapples with issues of guilt and finding resolution and acceptance through spiritual faith.

In Treatment (Season 1) – DVD

In Treatment, an intense half-hour drama set within the confines of individual psychotherapy sessions. Paul, a therapist, exhibits an insightful, confident demeanour when treating his patients, but presents with crippling insecurity when counselled by his own therapist. A compelling drama that examines what happens when the gifted therapist persona wears off and your own complexities are exposed.

MOVIES

Eat, Pray, Love (2010)

Elizabeth Gilbert decides to leave the trappings of American success to find herself. She sets out on a journey to study three different aspects of her nature with three different cultures; Gilbert explores the art of pleasure in Italy, the art of devotion in India, and then a balance between the two on the Indonesian island of Bali.

She learns that change doesn't happen on its own one day, but rather you have to be open to it. And sometimes that means decluttering your mind and your life, in order to make new for something new: your best possible, and happiest, self.

Love Happens (2009)

After losing his wife, Burke Ryan (Aaron Eckhart) writes a self-help book about coping with loss, except he doesn't really believe in it, himself. When he meets Eloise (Jennifer Aniston) he learns that letting go of regret, grief and preconceptions is perhaps the most crucial step to take if he wants to move forward with his life.

APPS

Mindmeister

Create mind maps for all your creative ideas; get them out of your head and onto a plan. File in different folders with assignments, tasks and attachments.

This is a great way to help clear your mind from ideas that better belong on "paper," anyway.

Evernote

Keep track of all ideas whether they are web pages, pictures, scribbles or notes, and access them via your computer or handheld devices.

This app is easily searchable and is designed with clear functionality, to help keep your mind, and your phone, uncluttered.

www.ingramcontent.com/pod-product-compliance
Lightning Source LLC
Chambersburg PA
CBHW060434220526
45465CB00008B/3139